DIY MONSTERS & MISCHIEF MAKERSPACE

MAKE A HAUNTED HOUSE YOUR WAY!

RACHAEL L. THOMAS

CONSULTING EDITOR,
DIANE CRAIG,
M.A./READING SPECIALIST

Super Sandcastle

An Imprint of Abdo Publishing
abdobooks.com

abdobooks.com

Printed in the United States of America, North Mankato, Minnesota
052020
092020

THIS BOOK CONTAINS RECYCLED MATERIALS

Design: Emily O'Malley, Mighty Media, Inc.
Production: Mighty Media, Inc.
Editor: Megan Borgert-Spaniol
Cover Photographs: Mighty Media, Inc.; Shutterstock Images
Interior Photographs: Dave Ginsberg/Flickr; iStockphoto; Leonard Pickel; Mighty Media, Inc.; Shutterstock Images

The following manufacturers/names appearing in this book are trademarks:
Duck Tape®, Westcott® KleenCut®

Library of Congress Control Number: 2019957661

Publisher's Cataloging-in-Publication Data
Names: Thomas, Rachael L., author.
Title: Make a haunted house your way! / by Rachael L. Thomas.
Description: Minneapolis, Minnesota : Abdo Publishing, 2021 | Series: DIY monsters & mischief makerspace | Includes online resources and index.
Identifiers: ISBN 9781532193170 (lib. bdg.) | ISBN 9781098211813 (ebook)
Subjects: LCSH: Handicraft for children--Juvenile literature. | Haunted houses--Juvenile literature. | Textile crafts--Juvenile literature. | Monsters--Juvenile literature. | Paper work--Juvenile literature. | Refuse as art material--Juvenile literature.
Classification: DDC 745.5--dc23

Super SandCastle™ books are created by a team of professional educators, reading specialists, and content developers around five essential components—phonemic awareness, phonics, vocabulary, text comprehension, and fluency—to assist young readers as they develop reading skills and strategies and increase their general knowledge. All books are written, reviewed, and leveled for guided reading and early reading intervention programs for use in shared, guided, and independent reading and writing activities to support a balanced approach to literacy instruction.

TO ADULT HELPERS

The projects in this book are fun and simple. There are just a few things to remember to keep kids safe. Some projects may use sharp or hot objects. Also, kids may be using messy supplies. Make sure they protect their clothes and work surfaces. Be ready to offer guidance during brainstorming and assist when necessary.

CONTENTS

BECOME A MAKER

A makerspace is like a laboratory. It's a place where ideas are formed and problems are solved. Kids like you create wonderful things in makerspaces. Many makerspaces are in schools and libraries. But they can also be in kitchens, bedrooms, and backyards. Anywhere can be a makerspace when you use imagination, inspiration, **collaboration**, and problem-solving!

IMAGINATION

This takes you to new places and lets you experience new things. Anything is possible with imagination!

INSPIRATION

This is the spark that gives you an idea. Inspiration can come from almost anywhere!

Makerspace Toolbox

COLLABORATION

Makers work together. They ask questions and get ideas from everyone around them. **Collaboration** solves problems that seem impossible.

PROBLEM—SOLVING

Things often don't go as planned when you're creating. But that's part of the fun! Find creative **solutions** to any problem that comes up. These will make your project even better.

MAKE SOME MISCHIEF!

When was the last time you made mischief? Mischief is playful behavior that's goofy or surprising. Mischief can take the form of a funny **prank** or teasing trick. You can also make mischief by decking your house with haunted surprises!

PROBLEM-SOLVE!
See page 26

HOUSE OF HORRORS

A haunted house is a maze of creepy creatures and objects. You can make any space feel haunted by adding a dash of the **supernatural**. Making your home spooky can be as simple as hanging huge cobwebs. You could also make mischief by hiding monsters in drawers and closets!

IMAGINE A HAUNTED HOUSE

A haunted house is like any home. But it's full of **supernatural** surprises! Monsters, ghosts, and creepy objects wait around every corner. Maybe you've seen haunted houses on TV and in movies. Or perhaps you've even visited one. In a makerspace, you can imagine and create the features of your very own haunted house!

GET INSPIRED!
See page 24

IMAGINE

If you could create any kind of haunted house, what mischief would take place inside? Would a ghost live in the closet? Would the TV turn on by itself? Would a hairy werewolf wait under the bed? Remember, there are no rules. Let your imagination run wild!

DESIGN A HAUNTED HOUSE

It's time to turn your idea into a makerspace marvel! Think about the things that will make your house haunted. Are there monsters with **fangs**, fur, or scales? Do household objects suddenly have minds of their own? How could you use the materials around you to create these haunted features? Where would you begin?

INSPIRATION

America's largest haunted house experience is called Terror Behind the Walls. It is built in an abandoned prison in Philadelphia, Pennsylvania. The creators of the experience carefully plan how to spook and scare visitors. The show includes hundreds of performers, special effects, and **mechanical** creatures!

COLLABORATE!
See page 28

BE SAFE, BE RESPECTFUL
MAKERSPACE ETIQUETTE

THERE ARE JUST A FEW RULES TO FOLLOW
WHEN YOU ARE CREATING YOUR HAUNTED HOUSE:

1. **ASK FOR PERMISSION AND ASK FOR HELP.** Make sure an adult says it's OK to make a haunted house. Get help using sharp tools, such as a craft knife, or hot tools, like a glue gun.

2. **THINK IT THROUGH.** Don't give up when things don't work out exactly right. Instead, think about the problem you are having. What are some ways to solve it?

3. **SHARE THE SPACE.** Share supplies and space with other makers. Put materials away when you are finished working. Find a safe space to store unfinished projects until next time.

4. **BE NICE.** Keep your tricks and **pranks** fun or funny, but not mean. Don't make your haunted house too scary for visitors. Mischief should be fun for everyone!

WHAT WILL HAUNT YOUR HOUSE?

Which places and spaces will you make haunted? Knowing this will help you figure out which materials to use.

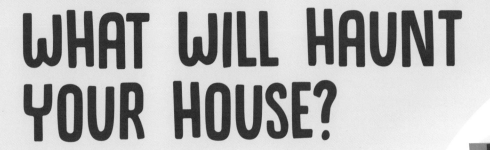

Will something reach out from under the bed?
Then you'll need a long handle for your monster's paw.

PROBLEM-SOLVE!
See page 26

IMAGINE

WHAT IF YOU WERE BUILDING A HAUNTED TREEHOUSE? HOW COULD YOU USE MATERIALS FROM NATURE TO MAKE YOUR LEAFY HOME CREEPY?

Will the dining room host a spooky feast? Then turn everyday snacks into a platter of **disgusting** delights!

Designer Leonard Pickel studied to be an **architect** in the 1970s. In 1987, he founded Hauntrepreneurs. This company builds spooky spaces in haunted houses. Pickel likes to create spaces that trick the eye and **unnerve** visitors. He calls his designs "darkitecture."

Will hallway paintings watch those who pass?

Then give your artwork **adjustable** eyes that can spy on visitors.

14

COLLABORATE!
See page 28

Will your front door warn visitors of what's to come? Then make a scary door knocker that can hang at the entrance.

⚠ STUCK?

YOU CAN ALWAYS CHANGE YOUR MIND IN A MAKERSPACE. CAN'T FIND THE RIGHT PIECES FOR A DOOR KNOCKER? HAVE YOUR HORRIFYING HEAD HANG FROM THE CEILING BY FISHING LINE!

15

CRAFT YOUR HAUNTED HOUSE

Turning your home into a haunted house takes planning. Think about which rooms are best for haunted tricks and **pranks**. You could decorate existing objects in those rooms. Or you could build something completely new!

SEARCH YOUR SPACE

The perfect material might be in a kitchen drawer, your school desk, or even your closet. Search for materials that might seem surprising!

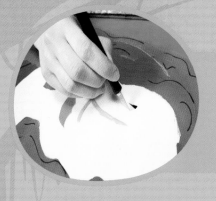

POSTER PAPER

WOOD DOWEL AND POOL NOODLE

GET INSPIRED!
See page 24

STRONG STRUCTURE

DOUGHNUT HOLES

GUMMY WORMS

EVERYTHING EDIBLE

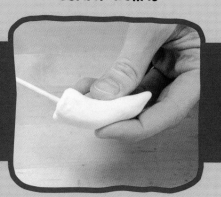

FOAM BRICK

AIR-DRY CLAY

SUPER SCULPTING

17

CONNECT YOUR CREEPY CREATIONS

Will you keep your haunted creations for a long time? Or will you take them apart after you are done scaring people? Knowing this will help you decide what materials to use.

TOTALLY TEMPORARY

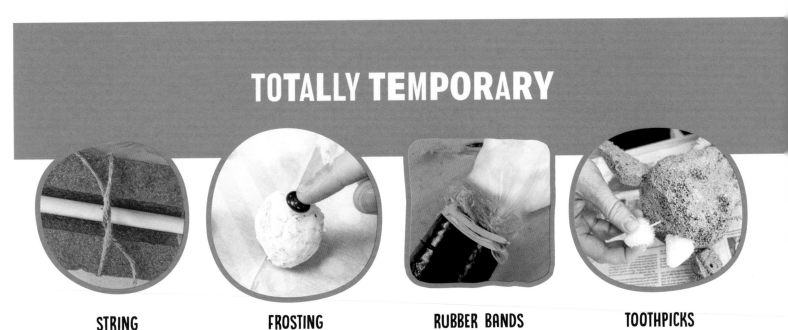

STRING   FROSTING   RUBBER BANDS   TOOTHPICKS

IMAGINE

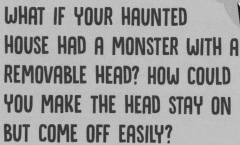

WHAT IF YOUR HAUNTED HOUSE HAD A MONSTER WITH A REMOVABLE HEAD? HOW COULD YOU MAKE THE HEAD STAY ON BUT COME OFF EASILY?

COLLABORATE!
See page 28

A LITTLE STICKY

SUPER STICKY

STAPLES

GLUE DOTS

DUCT TAPE

HOT GLUE

19

DECORATE YOUR CREEPY CREATIONS

Decorating is the final step in making your haunted house. It's where you add **details** to spook and surprise people. How do these decorations help bring your **designs** to life?

TISSUE PAPER AND CHENILLE STEMS

FAKE CREEPY-CRAWLIES

IMAGINE

WHAT IF YOUR HOUSE WERE HAUNTED BY AN INVISIBLE MONSTER? WHAT TRACES MIGHT IT LEAVE TO LET YOU KNOW IT'S THERE?

20

GET INSPIRED!
See page 24

DELICIOUSLY DISGUSTING

HAIR-RAISING

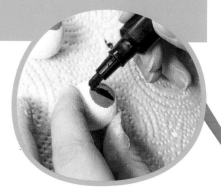

FOOD COLORING

GRAHAM CRACKERS

GEMS

MARKERS

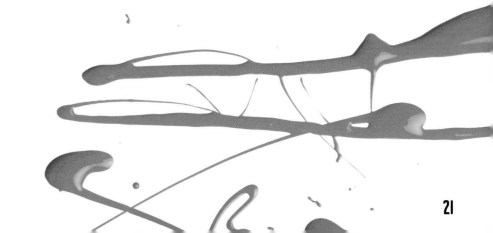

HELPFUL HACKS

As you work, you might discover ways to make challenging tasks easier. Try these simple tricks and **techniques** as you craft your haunted house!

Cut up glow stars for **fangs** that glow in the dark.

To make **edible** mealworms, first add water to frosting to make a sticky liquid. Coat gummy worms with the liquid. Then roll the worms in graham cracker crumbs!

PROBLEM-SOLVE!
See page 26

Fill a plastic baggie with frosting. Cut a small hole in the corner of the bag for piping the frosting.

A golf ball or other hard, lightweight object makes a good homemade door knocker.

⚠ STUCK?

MAKERS AROUND THE WORLD SHARE THEIR PROJECTS ON THE INTERNET AND IN BOOKS. IF YOU HAVE A MAKERSPACE PROBLEM, THERE'S A GOOD CHANCE SOMEONE ELSE HAS ALREADY FOUND A SOLUTION. SEARCH THE INTERNET OR LIBRARY FOR HELPFUL ADVICE AS YOU MAKE YOUR PROJECTS!

GET INSPIRED

Get inspiration from the real world before you start creating your haunted house!

LOOK AROUND YOUR HOME

Take a close look at the rooms in your house and the objects in each room. Living rooms often have sofas and TVs. Bedrooms often have closets, slippers, and pillows. Think about how you might make these everyday objects scary!

GO TO THE THEATER

Set **designers** often build walls, doors, and furniture for theater productions. Theaters also use special effects to surprise the audience. Actors can fly around the stage or disappear in a puff of smoke. How can you use set design and special effects in your haunted house?

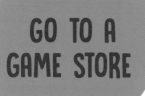

GO TO A GAME STORE

Role-playing games such as Dungeons and Dragons have players build their own scary scenes and stories. Go to your local game store to get ideas for your creation. Take a look at the books, **props**, and models on the shelves.

25

PROBLEM-SOLVE

No makerspace project goes exactly as planned. But with a little creativity, you can find a **solution** to any problem.

FIGURE OUT THE PROBLEM

Maybe the eyes of your haunted painting aren't staying in their eye sockets. Why do you think this is happening? Thinking about what is causing the problem can lead you to a solution!

SOLUTION:
SECURE THE EYES TO THE BACK
OF THE PAINTING USING A
TOOTHPICK AND TAPE.

BRAINSTORM AND TEST

Try coming up with three possible **solutions** to any problem.
Maybe you're having trouble attaching fur to your monster paw.
You could:

1. Use a stronger connector to attach the fur.

2. Use a lighter material for the fur.

3. Skip the fur and make a skeleton hand instead!

COLLABORATE

Collaboration means working together with others. There are tons of ways to collaborate to create a haunted house!

ASK A FELLOW MAKER

Don't be shy about asking a friend or classmate for help on your project. Other makers can help you think through the different steps to creating your haunted house. These helpers can also lend a hand during construction!

ASK AN ADULT HELPER

This could be a parent, teacher, grandparent, or any trusted adult. Tell this person about your dream haunted house. Your grown-up helper might think of materials or **techniques** you never would have thought of!

ASK AN EXPERT

An artist or **designer** can help you sketch your ideas for creepy creatures and features. An **architect** thinks about what makes houses comfortable and friendly. She or he could advise you on how to do the opposite too!

29

THE WORLD IS A MAKERSPACE!

Your haunted house may seem complete, but don't close your makerspace toolbox yet. Think about what would make your house even spookier. What would you do differently if you made it again? What would happen if you used different **techniques** or materials?

DON'T STOP AT HAUNTED HOUSES

You can use your makerspace toolbox beyond the makerspace! You might use it to accomplish everyday tasks, such as building a fort or icing a cake. But makers use the same toolbox to do big things. One day, these tools could help make movies or build museums. Turn your world into a makerspace! What problems could you solve?

GLOSSARY

adjust – to change something slightly to produce a desired result. An object is adjustable if it is designed to be used in more than one way.

architect – someone who designs buildings.

collaborate – to work with others.

design – to plan how something will appear or work. A design is a sketch or outline of something that will be made.

detail – a small part of something.

disgusting – creating a strong feeling of dislike toward something unpleasant or offensive.

edible – safe to eat.

fang – a long, pointed tooth.

invisible – unable to be seen.

mechanical – made or operated by a machine or tool.

prank – a trick done to someone as a joke.

prop – an object that is carried or used by an actor or a person playing a role.

solution – an answer to, or a way to solve, a problem.

supernatural – relating to magic, spirits, or other things that cannot be explained by science or nature.

technique – a method or style in which something is done.

unnerve – to make nervous or afraid.